SCHUBERT

Fantasy in C
'The Wanderer', D.760

Edited and annotated by
HOWARD FERGUSON

THE ASSOCIATED BOARD OF
THE ROYAL SCHOOLS OF MUSIC

INTRODUCTION

SOURCES

A Autograph, dated Nov. 1822. The title-page reads 'Fantaisie pour le Pianoforte composée et dediée à Monsieur Emm. Noble de Liebenberg de Zsittin par François Schubert mp.' (Vienna, Private Collection.) The whole of p.11, consisting of 7½ bars of the 2nd movement (i.e. from the 2nd half of b.44 to the end of b.51), has been stroked out and re-written on a separate sheet by someone other than the composer – possibly the publisher Diabelli. Schubert had completed the page, but with so many corrections and abbreviations that it would have been difficult for an engraver to decipher. Nevertheless, with care it is still possible to read almost all of it.

B The copyist's leaf mentioned above, now part of A. The recto consists of his copy of the 7½ bars stroked out in the 2nd movement. (The copy is not entirely accurate, as can be seen from footnote 6 to b.47 of the 2nd movement.) On the verso is what appears to be a sketch for the last 6 bars of an orchestral Menuet or Scherzo in A major or A flat (there is no key-signature). The barlines are drawn from the top stave to the bottom, but only the top stave (? Violin I) contains music.

C 1st edition: *Fantaisie pour le Piano-Forte composée et dediée à Monsieur Em: Noble de Liebenberg de Zittin par François Schubert.* *Oeuvre 15*; Cappi & Diabelli, Plate No.1174, Vienna [1823].

The present edition takes A as its main text, but adopts readings from C when they appear to have originated with the composer (see below). Differences between the two sources are listed in the footnotes.

THE TEXT

The precise relationship between A & C is unclear. A looks more like a first draft than a fair-copy; yet it contains a large number of engraver's marks, though not a complete set – there are only a few in the 1st movement. The layout of C follows them in the 4th movement and in some parts of the 2nd and 3rd, but not elsewhere. No other autograph is known. Though Schubert seems only rarely to have been given a chance to read proofs of his piano works, it looks as though this Fantasy was one of the exceptions: for, apart from obvious misprints, C differs from A in a number of details, some of which suggest the intervention of the composer. For example, in I, b.150, r.h. chord 3, the middle note in A is F, whereas it is E flat in C; in I, b.164, l.h. chord 1, the D is missing in A, but has been added in C; and in III, b.5, etc., r.h. notes 1-2 (and throughout the movement), the two-note slur is shown only in C.

STRUCTURE

The familiar title 'The Wanderer' does not stem from Schubert or any of his contemporaries. It is nevertheless appropriate, since the first eight bars of the 2nd movement consist of bb.23-30 (slightly modified) of the song 'Der Wanderer', D.489, written eight years earlier. Moreover, the rhythmic kernel of the passage (♩ ♫) appears in almost every theme of the Fantasy (I, bb.1 & 47; II, b.1; III, bb.3 & 79; IV, b.1), thus anticipating Liszt's favourite device of 'theme transformation'. Another 'Lisztian' trait (also found in the magnificent Fantasy in F minor, D.940, for piano duet) is the telescoping of what would normally be the separate movements of a sonata into a single continuous structure, in which the fourth 'movement' combines the functions of development and recapitulation of the first.

It might appear at first sight that the melody of I, bb.112-131, is completely new, thus suggesting rondo-form rather than sonata-form; but it is, of course, a development of bar 2 of the 2nd subject (I, b.47*f*). The slow movement (II) was neatly described by Donald Tovey as 'a kind of set of variations – because the variations all arise as so many continuations of a theme that has no end' (i.e. II, bb.1-8).

TEMPO

In movements I, II & III, as in many of Schubert's sonata-type works, more than a single tempo is needed in order to reflect the contrasted moods of the themes. The metronome marks suggested below are neither authoritative nor binding; but they will give some idea of how comparatively small (though important) the differences are likely to be. Where there is a musical link between two sections, the change of tempo is likely to be gradual (as in I, bb.68-69); when there is no link (as in I, b.132) it will perforce be abrupt.

I   Allegro con fuoco ma non troppo [♩ =c.132];
    b.47 [♩ =c.120]; b.70 [♩ =c.132];
    b.112 [♩ =c.120]; b.161 [♩ =c.108];
    b.165 [♩ =c.132].
II Adagio [♪=c.72]; b.18 [♪=c.80]; b.31 [♪=c.72];
    b.39 [♪=c.66].
III Presto [♩.=c.80]; b.79 [♩.=c.72]; b.95 [♩.=c.80];
    b.161 [♩.=c.72]; b.177 [♩.=c.80]; b.320 [♩.=c.72];
    b.342 [♩.=c.80].
IV Allegro [♩ =c.132].

These suggested markings do not, of course, include small local variations (rubatos) within the tempi, such as those required in the more reflective sections.

STACCATO DOTS (•) AND WEDGES (▾)

These two signs are clearly differentiated in the autograph. It seems likely that Schubert used the wedge in its pre-Beethoven sense of an accent, either with or without staccato. Dots generally appear here in conjunction with slurs, to indicate a mezzo-staccato; but in I, bb.112-131, III, bb.87-94 and 169-171, where they are shown on the initial note of l.h. broken-chord figures, they probably indicate a lightly accentuated note, as in the r.h. demi-semiquavers (32nd-notes) in Beethoven's Sonata in A flat, Op. 110, 1st movement, b.12*f*.

RHYTHMIC CONVENTIONS

The only place in the Fantasy where duple and triple rhythms occur simultaneously is in II, bb.27-34. Here it seems likely, however, that one should *not* follow the old convention of adjusting the former to coincide with the latter (as Schubert often intended), since the true duple rhythm of the r.h. melody has been established from the outset of the movement.

Ornaments

The only ornaments found in the Fantasy are arpeggios and single small notes.

Arpeggio: ⦚ . The sign appears only in II, bb.2 & 6, where it runs across the two staves and therefore implies a single arpeggio beginning (on the beat) with the lowest l.h. note and continuing upwards: i.e., *not* two separate arpeggios beginning simultaneously in the l.h. and r.h. Players who cannot stretch r.h. chord 4 in II, b.7 and chord 1 in b.8 should arpeggiate them as suggested in footnote (*a*).

Single small note: ♪ . Paul Badura-Skoda has pointed out that a single small note in the voice part of a Schubert song often stands for a long appoggiatura, whereas the same appoggiatura is shown in the piano accompaniment at its true value, i.e. as a normal-sized note. Hence it would appear that in the piano works a single small note (of whatever value) is usually intended to be a short, unaccented acciaccatura (the present-day ♪). In I, r.h. bb.124-127 (the only times the ornament appears here) the problem is: should the small notes be played *on* the 'beat', or before it? It is particularly hard to decide, since both versions are awkward in bb.124-125 because of collisions, or near-collisions, with the l.h. Since no definite ruling can be given, the player should experiment with both interpretations, and choose whichever he finds the more convincing. In either case he will find it helpful to keep the hand close to the keys, and to think of each pair as a stretch rather than a leap.

This Edition

In the present edition numbered footnotes are concerned with textual matters, and lettered footnotes with the interpretation of ornaments, etc. Redundant accidentals have been omitted. Editorial accidentals, notes, rests, dynamics, etc., are printed either in small type or within square brackets, and editorial slurs, ties, and 'hairpin' *cresc*. and *dim*. signs are crossed with a small vertical line. Curved brackets indicate that a note should not be struck. The fingering throughout is editorial, as there is none in the sources.

Schubert's distribution of notes on the two staves appears to have been dictated by scribal convenience rather than musical or pianistic considerations: like many earlier composers, his aim was to avoid so far as possible the use of leger-lines and clef changes. The result is often confusing for the player: for at times the whole texture is crammed on to a single stave, and chords and melodies lose their visual shape through being divided between the two staves. The editor has therefore felt free to alter the layout whenever doing so might make it easier to read. Generally his aim has been to place r.h. notes on the upper stave and l.h. notes on the lower; but occasionally it has been more convenient to use the signs ⌊ and ⌈ to indicate the r.h. and l.h. respectively.

HOWARD FERGUSON
Cambridge 1980

FANTASY in C
('The Wanderer')
D.760

SCHUBERT
November 1822

Allegro con fuoco ma non troppo

(a) semiquavers, not *tremolando*.

1) B.5, r.h. note 5: A & C have staccato-dash to C sharps; but see b.2, etc.

2) B.14, C mistakenly has ⟩.

3) B.27, last three quavers to b.31, first five quavers: in A these 4 bars were added as an afterthought at the foot of the page.

A.B.1783

4) B.37 r.h: C continues the crotchet stems on notes 1,5,9 & 13; but they would be better on notes 3,7,11 & 15, as in bb. 43-44.

(b) gracenote before the beat.
5) B.79, r.h. beat 2: crotchet in both A & C; but see more probable bb. 10, 12 & 81.

6) B.102, l.h. final chord, lowest note: E in A, D in C.
7) B.103: *p* in C; none in A.

(c) gracenotes either before the 'beat', or thus :-
(See the preliminary Notes, under Ornamentation.)

8) B.132: *f* in C; indistinct in A — could be either *f* or *ff*.

9) B 142, r.h. chord 4: thus in C; in A

A.B.1783

12

10) B.145, l.h. note 13: in C the flat is missing to the E.
11) B.150, r.h. chord 3, middle note: F in A; in C, F altered to E flat.

A.B.1783

12) B.164, l.h. chord 1: thus in C, D missing in A.

Adagio

(a) for small hands:

(b) demi-semiquavers, not *tremolando*.

1) B. 23: *fp* in C; indistinct in A — could be *ff*, which seems more probable.
2) B. 25: *decresc.* in C; ditto in A, but with *p* on beat 1.

(C) for small hands: omit the r.h. B (sharp) below the A sharp, and play the F (sharp) with the 3rd finger.
3) B.32, l.h. final group, two lower notes: three semiquavers in both A & C — doubtless a slip by Schubert.
4) B.37, r.h. beat 3: thus in A; C omits the three G s.

5) B.44, 2nd half to end of b.51: see Preliminary Note on Source B. Possibly there should be a *fp* here, to allow for the *cresc.* in b.45.

6) B.47, beat 3: both B & C have the r.h. rhythm ♪·♪♪♪♪·♪♪♪ ; and omit the *ffz* on beat 4.

7) B.49, r.h. beat 3: thus in both A & B; C has ♪·♪ , probably mistakenly.

8) B.52, r.h. beat 3: A has ♩· ♪ (i.e. with one dot), C ♩· ♪; but see b.49.

9) B.56, l.h. note 33: D natural in A; no natural in C.

Presto

(a) for small hands: omit the r.h.Fs. (But if this is done, the r.h. A(flats) in b.15 should *also* be omitted, in order to balance the two passages.)
1) Bb. 5,11, etc., r.h. notes 1-2: the 2-note slur here and elsewhere is shown only in C.
2) Bb.19-22: Schubert added these 4 bars in the margin, to replace two stroked-out bars.

3) B.58, r.h. chord 2: B (flat) missing in both A & C; but see b.30.
4) B.79: dynamics thus in A; in C the l.h. *p* is missing.
5) B.98, r.h. note 4: thus in A; C has a flat to the D, probably mistakenly.

6) Bb. 151-152: by writing the low F flats Schubert inadvertently exceeded the downward compass of his piano by a semitone.

7) B.158, r.h. chord 1: thus in C; A omits the lower B (flat). Chord 2: thus in C; A mistakenly has F as the top note.
8) B.167, l.h. chord 2: thus in both A & C; but the equivalent b. 85 would make the top note D (flat) instead of B(flat).

9) Bb. 330-331, r.h: thus in A; C mistakenly duplicates bb. 328-329.
10) B. 346: C has *fz* on beat 1; mistakenly duplicating b. 345.

Allegro

1) B.1: *f* in A; *ff* in C.
2) B.33, r.h. chord 3: in both A & C the top note is G. This seems to have been a slip on Schubert's part, like the similar one in III/b.158.
   In a fugal texture the sudden increase from three parts (discounting doublings) to four is unlikely; moreover, a G would awkwardly an-
   ticipate the G in the following bars.

(a) semiquavers, not *tremolando*.
3) B.62, r.h. note 9: E in both A & C —obviously a slip.

4) B.77, r.h. chord 1: thus in C; in A the B flat is missing.
5) Bb. 82, 84, 86, 88, 89 and beat 1 of 90: in A the l.h. is written

32

Printed in England by Caligraving Limited Thetford Norfolk

A.B.1783